S0-BHX-884

E. M. Forster

by HARRY T. MOORE

Columbia University Press

NEW YORK *&* LONDON 1965

HARRY T. MOORE is a Research Professor at Southern Illinois University. He is the author of a number of books, including *The Life and Works of D. H. Lawrence,* and editor of *The World of Lawrence Durrell, Selected Letters of Rainer Maria Rilke,* and *Collected Letters of D. H. Lawrence,* among others. Professor Moore is a Fellow of the Royal Society of Literature.

Copyright © 1965 Columbia University Press
Library of Congress Catalog Card Number: 65–16383
Manufactured in the United States of America

6460

E. M. Forster

E. M. Forster has written five novels, two of them of major importance; enough short stories to make up a moderate-sized "Collected" volume; and a series of miscellaneous books and articles, sometimes related to the fiction and sometimes independent exercises in belles-lettres. Forster's principal writings concern the failure of human beings to communicate with one another satisfactorily, their failure to smash down the walls of prejudice that have risen between them and to establish among themselves the relationships that are so richly possible.

Given a wider application, this is the history of humanity in our time. Forster, beginning his work early in this century of wars, saw from the first the schisms between people and between the separate worlds they live in. But if his works are prophetic, they are not prescriptively so. The value of his fiction lies to a great extent in his representative portraits of people.

Forster ardently believes in the right of every member of humanity to be as much himself as he can be within the bounds of community safety. As a supporter of a political system that grants each of us his uniqueness, Forster is willing to give democracy two cheers at least: "Two cheers are quite enough: there is no occasion to give three. Only Love the Beloved Republic deserves that." Yet that republic cannot function effectively in a climate of prejudices and antagonisms. On the title page of one of his two finest novels, *Howards End* (1910), Forster placed a phrase representing the philosophy of

[3]

one of his characters, which is essentially his own philosophy: "Only connect."

Forster was born in 1879, the son of a London architect who died when the boy was two years old. His education, his enjoyment of leisure time, as well as his ability to undertake his earlier travels ("and travelling inclined me to write") were all made possible by a legacy from his great-aunt, Marianne Thornton, who died when Forster was eight. Before attending the university, however, he had to undergo the torment of being a day student at Tonbridge School, which seemed to him a concentration of injustice and misery. The wonder and freedom of Cambridge were a happy contrast, perhaps best summed up in Forster's novel *The Longest Journey* (1907) and in his 1934 biography of Goldsworthy Lowes Dickinson.

During his first four years at Cambridge, 1897–1901, Forster barely knew Dickinson, who was sixteen years older. Forster had intended to study with him, but was "dished by Oscar Browning," the fat and sharp-minded history teacher, who said, "You must come to me." Forster's classics tutor was the forceful Nathaniel Wedd, of whom he wrote in the 1934 Dickinson biography: "It is to him more than to Dickinson—indeed more to him than to anyone—that I owe such awakening as has befallen me. It is through him that I can best imagine the honesty and fervor of fifty years back." There was conscious honesty and concentrated fervor at Cambridge in Forster's time in the person and philosophy of G. E. Moore, whose *Principia Ethica* became highly popular at the university after its publication in 1903. Moore, who stressed that the "good" was indefinable and who searched intently for the exact meaning of every statement, had an immense influence on undergraduates of the period, particularly in the circle in which Forster moved.

In 1901–2 Forster made his first visit to Italy and Greece and

[4]

began writing short fiction and novels. The first novel to be published was *Where Angels Fear to Tread* (1905), followed by *The Longest Journey* (1907), *A Room with a View* (1908), *Howards End* (1910), and long after, by *A Passage to India* (1924). His first volume of shorter work, *The Celestial Omnibus and Other Stories*, came out in 1911; *The Eternal Moment and Other Stories* appeared in 1928 (all the tales had been written before World War I). The nonfiction volumes began with Forster's guidebook to Alexandria in 1922. Before the war, Forster had become part of the Bloomsbury group, whose members included the daughters of Sir Leslie Stephen, Virginia (later Mrs. Woolf) and Vanessa (later Mrs. Bell), and their brothers, Adrian and Thoby, as well as J. M. Keynes, Lytton Strachey, Leonard Woolf, Clive Bell, Roger Fry, Duncan Grant, David Garnett, and several others prominent in London intellectual and artistic life.

In 1910 Forster returned to Cambridge for his M.A. He spent the winter of 1912–13 in India, accompanied part of the time by Dickinson. After war broke out, Forster volunteered for the Red Cross, which sent him to Alexandria, where he remained from 1915 to 1918. In 1922 he returned to India for six months as private secretary to the Maharajah of the State of Dewas Senior. In 1927 Forster became a fellow of his old college, King's. Since World War II, he has again traveled frequently—to South Africa, the United States, Italy, and Greece—but has spent most of his time in residence at King's.

Although E. M. Forster may not have had an outwardly eventful life, this shy and gentle man has lived intensely through adventures of the spirit: knowledge, personal relationships, a love of certain places, and the satisfaction of writing. Forster was not widely read even after *A Passage to India*, but his reputation has grown steadily, particularly since World War II. Although he has not brought out a novel for more than forty years, he is, at this moment of writing, generally regarded as England's finest living novelist.

Before specific consideration of Forster's nonfiction works and his five novels, we may take his short stories as a good starting point for a discussion of his writing career. The outstanding characteristic of these stories should be noted at once: they are almost entirely given over to fantasy, mythology, magic, the supernatural. These elements are sometimes at the edge of Forster's novels, and in *A Passage to India* there is a suggestion that they have made a definite invasion; yet the novels for the most part are in the vein of everyday realism. They are pointed up by the comic and the ironic, but they remain largely within the area of the realistic (though rarely the naturalistic). This is to say that the novels proceed at the pace of probability; some of the episodes may seem melodramatic, some of the people may dip over into caricature, and some of the episodes may be tinged with mystery, yet in the main the books are about life as we confront it each morning, not always necessarily making in our minds a clear distinction between its real and apparent aspects, but accepting its surface manifestations within the scope of the probable and the predictable. Forster's short stories, on the other hand, are not like this. We may meet in any of them a group of plausible people, and they may say what we might expect them to say, but there is always the tense possibility that, without warning, a poltergeist will start tumbling the furniture about. No reader is quite "safe" in a Forster short story.

Still another aspect of his work in this medium should be noted. The themes are essentially those of the novels. In other words, Forster in the short stories adopts the guise of fantasy to put across what he says realistically in his longer fiction. As one example, consider the fate of Mr. Bons in the story "The Celestial Omnibus." He is a man with pretensions, who, al-

[6]

though he has no genuine love of poetry, keeps fancy editions of the poets. In one of Forster's novels, Mr. Bons would have been mocked at or would have suffered some spiritual defeat. But when Dante (yes, Dante) is driving Mr. Bons in the celestial omnibus, Bons is horribly punished for his literalness, dropped from a great height and smashed. Here, fantasy in a most unusual way combines with a naturalistic event. But fantasy is at the basis of the destruction, whereas it would not have been in one of the novels.

The first story that Forster wrote he placed at the beginning of *The Celestial Omnibus* and also of *The Collected Tales of E. M. Forster* (British edition, *Collected Short Stories*). In "The Story of a Panic," some English people picnicking in the Italian countryside are suddenly seized by terror, and flee. If the spirit of panic has entered into their systems, the spirit of Pan has taken over that of the fourteen-year-old Eustace, whose ecstasies cause his elders to lock him up in a small room at the hotel. A young Italian waiter, Gennaro, who is the only one capable of understanding what has happened, protests that Eustace will die if he is imprisoned. Gennaro, who has betrayed Eustace into captivity for ten lire, finally sets him free, and as Eustace rushes away toward the woodland uttering strange cries, Gennaro says, "Now, instead of dying, he will live!"—but Gennaro himself falls dead.

This is typical Forster fantasy, recurring in slightly different fashion in another of the stories in *The Celestial Omnibus*, "Other Kingdom." Here, Evelyn Beaumont has been brought to England from "uncivilized" Ireland to marry the handsome, stuffy, wealthy Harcourt Worters. But after experiencing the rigidity of his ideas, she makes an Ovidian flight and takes a dryad's refuge in a grove of trees. Another of Forster's stories contrasting the pettiness of the everyday world with another and better world, "The Other Side of the Hedge" is less successful, partly because its symbolism depends too much upon the methodical and too little upon the intuitive, and partly because the fable contains no true basis of dramatic conflict.

Several of the stories deal with the afterlife, at least with another world in close relationship to the present one. These include "The Celestial Omnibus," already mentioned, "The Point of It," "Mr. Andrews," and "Co-ordination." "The Celestial Omnibus" has something more to offer than the destruction of Mr. Bons (look at that name backwards and it becomes Snob): there is also a small boy with an eagerly imaginative mind who rides the omnibus and does not fall into (or fall in) the sin of literalness. Altogether, it is Forster's most charming story of the relation between the present world and eternity. "As for 'The Point of It,'" Forster says, "it was ill-liked when it came out by my Bloomsbury friends. 'What *is* the point of it?' they queried, nor did I know how to reply." But it seems to have several points. One of them is that Harold, who dies young, in glory (the text suggests the choice of Achilles), has the better of it, in contrast with his surviving friend Michael, who leads a long life devoted to humanity and the accumulation of honors. At death he finds himself in the soft hell of the humanists, separated from his wife, who is in the stony hell of the truth seekers; but there is a way out, the heaven of youth, if one can in an intense moment realize the point of it. "Mr. Andrews" is a brief, light allegory of an Englishman who finds that he and a Turk can enter paradise together and have everything they ask for, which is just a little too good, so they abandon heaven for the struggle of living again; they have, in the course of their meeting, achieved a new understanding and tolerance in that each has prayed that the other might be admitted to heaven. In "Co-ordination," the brevity again helps, and it sustains a light anecdote Forster knows better than to draw out: Beethoven and Napoleon cast, from the afterlife, an influence over a girls' school. The influence seems on the surface beneficent, but it is channeled through a series of confusions that make the final effect one of amusing irony.

In the vein of "The Story of a Panic," two other tales project mischief from the invisible world: "The Curate's Friend" and "The Story of the Siren." The title of "The Curate's Friend" seems at one level ironic, since the faun that appears to a Wiltshire curate, though not to those about him, breaks up the romance between the cleric and his fiancée; but the faun is in the longer view his friend, since the clergyman becomes, in his own eyes at least, a better man and a better clergyman. In "The Story of the Siren," a young boatman tells an English tourist the story of his brother Giuseppe, who had seen the Siren and had married Maria, who had also beheld the wonder. When Maria became pregnant, a priest murdered her: the child of this pagan-visioned Joseph and Mary must not be allowed to become the new non-Christian messiah. Giuseppe wandered over the world, his brother says, trying to find someone else who had seen the Siren, particularly a woman—for then a child could be created. But Giuseppe at last arrived at Liverpool ("Is the district probable?" his brother asks), where he became ill, and died coughing blood. The boatman says, "Silence and loneliness cannot last for ever. It may be a hundred or a thousand years, but the sea lasts longer, and she shall come out of it and sing." So ends the last-written and the finest of Forster's mythological stories, one that concentrates various themes of all the others, especially his preoccupation with the natural world (as represented by his vital Mediterranean figures), linked with the supernatural or mythological (here the Siren) against the false world of society (the priest and Giuseppe's conventional fellow Sicilians). The darkening grotto, the fanatical murder, and the wild sea in which the Siren lives all combine to give the story its particular force.

[9]

In "The Machine Stops," Forster made a somewhat similar statement in a quite different way: he showed how one element of the modern social complex—the machine—had triumphed over the natural life of man. Forster has spoken of the story as "a reaction to one of the earlier heavens of H. G. Wells." But it is far more pessimistic than anything by Wells, and reflects none of his faith in science as it portrays a dehumanized world of the future. One of the earliest science-fiction stories, it was a forerunner of Aldous Huxley's *Brave New World* and, with the big-brother functioning of the machine, the tale also anticipated George Orwell's *1984*.

Forster in "The Road from Colonus" wrote in a fairly realistic vein, though the story has mysterious overtones, particularly in relation to an ironic coincidence. The elderly Mr. Lucas, on tour in Greece, finds a place at which he wants to stop, where in a dry landscape water gushes out of a hollow tree. But this Oedipus is not permitted to linger: his daughter enlists the aid of a young man in the touring party to carry her father gently away. Later, back in London, when the daughter is about to be married, apparently to the young man from the touring party, she discovers from an old newspaper that a huge tree had blown down at the place where her father had wanted to stop, and had killed all the people there. But Mr. Lucas hardly seems interested in the accident, for he is too deeply concerned over having to give up his house: he continually hears the gush of water, "and I cannot stand the noise of running water."

"The Eternal Moment," the best of Forster's short stories, begins with a situation that suggests Henry James, an author for whom Forster has expressed distaste. But the idea of the once-simple town (then in Italia Irredenta) which has become hideously commercialized because it was the setting of a popular novel, is intrinsically Jamesian. Forster works it out, however, as James would not have: the story becomes another account of those failures of people to reach one another from their different worlds. Miss Raby, an aging spinster novelist, returns to Vorta (based on Cortina d'Ampezzo) to see what damage her book has really done. Colonel Leyland, a fairly sophisticated and tolerant member of his class, is the platonic traveling companion of this woman given to heedless plain speaking. She tells him that years before one of the porters at the hotel where she lodged had tried to make love to her on the mountainside, and that she had promptly rejected him.

At Vorta they find that new and grand hotels have pushed into the background the charming little place where she had stayed. And the once-handsome porter, Feo, has become the swaggering fat concierge of the most swaggering and fattest of the new hotels. The candid Miss Raby mentions to Feo the mountainside scene, which he finally remembers with shock and embarrassment, and he fears, unreasonably, that she plans to blackmail him. On learning that he is married and has three small sons, she offers to export one of them to England, to adopt and educate him. Feo, who has no feeling for the child beyond wondering how much Miss Raby will pay for taking him, withdraws by saying his wife might object: the proper world he now represents as the concierge at the Hôtel des Alpes, whose personnel have been watching and listening during this scene, can have no dealings with the plainspoken Englishwoman who cries out in the hotel lounge, "Don't think I'm in love with you now!" But she had been when she rejected him, and in a blazing revelation she sees that episode on the mountain as perhaps the greatest moment of her life, the eternal moment from which she has drawn all her subsequent inspirations. But she has now lost Colonel Leyland, who touches his forehead so that Feo will see the gesture; and Feo whispers, "Exactly, sir. Of course we understand." Whatever

[11]

else has happened to her, however, Miss Raby has learned how to face old age. Leyland, who had seemed enlightened above his milieu, slips safely back into it. Henry James would have probably ended on a different note, full of those illuminating subtleties which make up for the lack of certain other elements in his work; Forster in that final scene in the lounge achieved a marvelous dramatic vigor.

The style of these stories, like that of the novels, is one of forceful simplicity. It was Forster's manner almost as much as his matter that aroused the enthusiasm of young English writers of the 1930s: Christopher Isherwood, W. H. Auden, and other members of the group of new young radicals of the day. Cyril Connolly said admiringly in *Enemies of Promise* (1939) that Forster had broken away from the "mandarin" style of such writers as Walter Pater, Henry James, and Joseph Conrad: Forster tends to use everyday words and to avoid conjunctive and relative clauses. Although he has not been imitated, Connolly says, Forster was the stylistic forerunner of Virginia Woolf, Katherine Mansfield, Elizabeth Bowen, and David Garnett. One of these writers, Elizabeth Bowen, has pointed out (in *Collected Impressions*, 1950) that the prose of Forster's essays resembles that of his fiction: "Its rhythm is so inherent in its content that one cannot detect it without analysis. The least frigid of writing, it is the most impersonal; [Forster] is the enemy of all those lovable little tricks."

Alexandria: A History and a Guide (1922) came out of Forster's experiences in that city during World War I. It is one of those special-interest books which can be read with enjoyment for its own sake; that is, by those who know little or nothing about Alexandria and have no particular intention of going there. The history section that takes up nearly half the book is a well-informed and colorful survey of the city from its founding in 331 B.C. to the riots and bombardment of A.D. 1882, when the British moved in. Earlier, Egyptians, Greeks, Romans, Arabs, and the armies of Napoleon cross the pages of the book. Its guide section is thorough, with street maps and plans of important monuments and temples. Forster dealt with Alexandria again in *Pharos and Pharillon* (1923), a series of sketches named for two lighthouses of the city: "Under [the vast and heroic] Pharos I have grouped a few antique events; to modern events and to personal impressions I have given the name of Pharillon, the obscure successor of Pharos, which clung for a time to the low rock of Silsileh and then slid unobserved into the Mediterranean." *Pharos and Pharillon* is a continuation of the history-guidebook; most of its sketches reaffirm Forster's Hellenism and his dislike of Christianity. They are often done in the mischievous vein of Anatole France, and at times they foreshadow a quite different kind of writer, the Lawrence Durrell of the *Alexandria Quartet.*

In 1927, three years after Forster's last novel (*A Passage to India*), he brought out his volume of expository criticism, *Aspects of the Novel,* originally delivered in that year as the Clark lectures at Trinity College, Cambridge. The book is best known for its distinction between the types of characters Forster calls "round" and "flat": "The test of a round character is that it is capable of surprising in a convincing way. If it never surprises, it is flat. It it does not convince, it is a flat pretending to be round." Forster elaborates on these ideas. Flat characters—humours, types, caricatures—are useful to the novelist, though they are not the great achievement that round characters are. The flat are best when comic, and more of them could have been profitably used, Forster thinks, in the great Russian novels. His own particular interests appear in the chapters on fantasy and prophecy, and in the one on "Pattern and Rhythm," in which he speaks of "the three large blocks of sound" that make up Beethoven's Fifth Symphony. Forster wonders whether there is any analogy to this type of rhythm in fiction. Although he says he knows of none, his own novels sometimes have this three-part pattern, and he has given the nod to at least one interpretation (Peter Burra's) of these books as "symphonic." Forster also has much to say, in *Aspects*, that is illuminating on the subject of plot and piquant on the subject of other novelists. Forster here wrote one of the first commentaries on Herman Melville's *Billy Budd* (in 1951 he was to prepare the libretto for Benjamin Britten's operatic version of *Billy Budd*). *Aspects of the Novel* is valuable not only for what it tells of Forster's ways and means of writing, but it is also an important study of the art of fiction.

Besides a number of short essays on the lives of authors, Forster has written two full-length biographies: *Goldsworthy Lowes Dickinson* (1934) and *Marianne Thornton* (1956). Both these books were in a way acts of piety, the first to commemorate a good friend, the second a beloved relative. The Dickinson volume, which came out two years after its subject's death, will mainly catch the attention of those concerned with Forster or with the Cambridge of yesterday and the day before. Dickinson's life is in the outward sense unchallenging to a biographer, since it can be only an intellectual record. Dickinson had a fine intellect: *The Greek View of Life* (1896) is still a useful and readable book, and the same may be said of his subsequent imaginary letters and dialogues. It is even, Forster says, "possible that Dickinson invented the phrase 'League of Nations,' " and he certainly did significant work for that organization. But, since his biography must be an intellectual treatise, it suffers somewhat because its subject's mind was not of the first and highest order.

On the other hand, *Marianne Thornton,* 1797–1887: *A Domestic Biography*, is, despite its modest subtitle, a compelling story. It is exciting to learn that Forster knew this woman who was born in the eighteenth century. His great-aunt was a member of the Clapham Sect of evangelicals, and the family knew Thomas Babington Macaulay, Bishop Wilberforce, and other famous men of the Victorian era. Forster's history of this branch of his family, with the full-length portrait of his great-aunt "Monie," is an attractive addition to the history of Victorian manners.

Forster collected many of his miscellaneous writings—articles, along with pamphlets and other small books—in *Abinger Harvest* (1936) and *Two Cheers for Democracy* (1951). The first of these books takes its name from the Surrey village where Forster lived for a number of years until he moved permanently to Cambridge after World War II. The volume includes *The Pageant of Abinger*, first performed in 1934 (music by Ralph Vaughan Williams), a series of episodes relating to the life of the town from the Middle Ages to modern times. In its Epilogue, the Woodman says, "Houses and bungalows, hotels, restaurants and flats, arterial roads, by-passes, petrol pumps and pylons—are these going to be England? Are these man's final triumph? Or is there another England, green and eternal, which will outlast them?"

The essays in *Abinger Harvest* are of various kinds, chiefly belletristic, with articles on Joseph Conrad, T. S. Eliot, Marcel Proust, and other authors, including Forster's great ideal, Jane Austen. Sometimes the chapters are personal, as the one devoted to a bit of family history: "Battersea Rise" tells something about the Thornton home, dealt with more expansively in *Marianne Thornton*. "Notes on the English Character" is just that, a series of notes neatly discussing well-known attributes and at one point providing an instructive comparison with Indian character. Nearly a third of the book comprises essays on the Orient, from Marco Polo to the situation of modern India. Lionel Trilling, usually an admirer of Forster's, finds some of the literary sketches coy, especially those dealing with Gibbon, Coleridge, and Keats; these pieces seem to have been influenced by Lytton Strachey's manner. But usually Forster is strictly himself in this book, never more so than in that Epilogue to *The Pageant of Abinger:*

If you want to ruin our Surrey fields and woodlands it is easy to do, very easy, and if you want to save them they can be saved. Look into your hearts and look into the past, and remember that all this beauty is a gift which you can never replace, which no money can buy, which no cleverness can refashion.

Here is the true Forster speaking. In some ways, although his manner is quite different, he resembles D. H. Lawrence, who also, but more violently, disliked the encroachment of civilization, and who also in his fiction opposed Anglo-Saxon philistines with vitalistic types reminiscent of such figures as the young Italian, Gino, in Forster's first novel, *Where Angels Fear to Tread.*

Forster's *Two Cheers for Democracy* is a miscellany similar to *Abinger Harvest*, though its opening section, "The Second Darkness"—devoted to the author's pamphlets and broadcasts during World War II—gives the book a somewhat different tone. These pieces are dated now except as examples of the kind of intellectual leadership a writer can provide during a time of crisis: Forster spoke out sanely against race theories, Nazism, and various other manifestations of the period. The belletristic essays that make up the rest of the book are some of Forster's finest, often adapted from reviews or occasional journalism but always sieved through a civilized and alert intelligence. The 1941 Rede lecture at Cambridge, in memory of Virginia Woolf, is a helpful examination of her work but, even more important, it is a knowledgeable presentation of her attitudes toward her work.

[16]

The other literary essays indicate the range of Forster's interests, from John Skelton to Gabriele D'Annunzio, while the travel sketches ("America is rather like life. You can usually find in it what you look for") are wittily perceptive, including "India Again" (1946), describing Forster's third visit there, and some informative English views, both London and Cambridge as well as T. E. Lawrence's Clouds Hill cottage and "The Last of Abinger." But *Two Cheers for Democracy* is best known for the essay "What I Believe," from a phrase of whose text the title was taken. Forster says he does not believe in Belief, though in an age of no faith and many militant creeds, one is compelled in self-defense to formulate one's own creed. "My law-givers are Erasmus and Montaigne, not Moses and St. Paul." He distrusts Great Men, who "produce a desert of uniformity around them, and often a pool of blood too." Forster continually keeps the emphasis on the individual and the personal: "If I had to choose between betraying my country and betraying my friend, I hope I should have the guts to betray my country."

It may seem a long leap back, from this point, to 1905 and Forster's first published novel, *Where Angels Fear to Tread*— and yet it is not really a very great leap because the novels and the stories, as well as even the later essays, are closely related, as a study of the novels will show. And they should properly be given the emphasis of last place, as the most important part of Forster's career.

Where Angels Fear to Tread begins on an irony, as the widowed Lilia Herriton is departing for Italy. "Love and understand the Italians," her brother-in-law, Philip Herriton, tells her at the end of the third paragraph of the story. She does not understand the Italians, but she soon falls in love with one of them. Caroline Abbott, her companion on what was to have been a long though temporary visit, telegraphs to the Herritons that the young man belongs to the nobility. This news is received skeptically; to the elder Mrs. Herriton it makes no difference whether the man is a duke or an organ-grinder. Philip goes out to Italy upon the command of his imperious mother: "If Lilia marries him she insults the memory of Charles, she insults Irma [her small daughter], she insults us." In an opening chapter of less than eighteen pages, Forster has, with deft strokes of social comedy, drawn the battle lines and provided at least rudimentary portraits of all the leading characters except Lilia's Italian, Gino Carella.

Philip, the stiff young barrister, has been to Italy before and has loved it. He is an ineffectual youth with two outstanding characteristics, a sense of beauty and a sense of humor. But the sense of beauty is a kind of embittered *bovarisme*, the disease of the provincial who dislikes his province but must live in it. And the sense of humor has become an acrid cynicism. Arriving in Italy, Philip finds out to his dismay that Lilia has already married; she is thirty-three, Gino twenty-one. But Philip has been even more horrified to learn that Gino is the son of a dentist: "False teeth and laughing gas and the tilting chair at a place which knew the Etruscan League, and the Pax Romana, and Alaric himself, and the Countess Matilda, and the Middle Ages, all fighting and holiness, and the Renaissance, all fighting and beauty!"

Philip returns home, accompanied by the rueful Caroline Abbott. The story then takes up Lilia's marriage, and her gradual disillusionment with Italian life. Gino, a sexual anarchist ("I always desired a blonde"), is soon being unfaithful. He keeps Lilia as his wife, however, for his deepest need is to have a son. Lilia dies giving birth to that son, dies in a single sentence with the abruptness that so often marks the death of Forster characters. Before long, Irma begins to receive picture postcards supposedly from her "lital brother." Mrs. Herriton orders Philip to Italy again, to "rescue" the baby, and with him she sends his priggish sister Harriet.

In Italy they meet Miss Abbott, who also feels responsible for the child; when Philip asks her whether she has come as traitor or spy, she takes no offense at the offensive words and admits she is there as a spy. She says that Mrs. Herriton, who cares nothing about the baby (which indeed is not even related to her), has behaved dishonorably; if her son and daughter really want to get it, however, Caroline will help, and if they want to fail, she will take the child. Later she withdraws altogether, telling Philip that if the little boy stays in Italy, with his loving father, he will be brought up badly, and that if he goes to England he will be brought up well, although nobody there loves him.

Gino in any event is not selling: he expects to marry a woman he does not love, but she has a little money and will be a mother to Lilia's baby. When Harriet grimly steals the child, she deepens the wrong by leading Philip to believe that she has bought him. Here, Philip the barrister proves to be poor at cross-examination, although the circumstances are admittedly against him, since he and Harriet are hurrying to the railway station in a carriage on a rain-swept night, and the baby is obviously ill. The carriage overturns, killing the child. Philip, with a broken elbow, goes to tell the news to Gino, who savagely twists Philip's fractured arm and begins to strangle him; he is saved only by the timely appearance of Caroline Abbott, who restores Gino to common sense and even a manifestation of friendship for Philip. When the housekeeper brings a jug of milk intended for the baby, Gino insists that Philip take it; and what Philip leaves, Gino ritually drinks.

On the way back to England, Philip starts to tell Caroline

[19]

that he is in love with her—oddly enough, these two old friends still address each other as Mr. Herriton and Miss Abbott—but she forestalls him by confessing that she is in love with Gino, "crudely" though profoundly. She will keep him in her memory forever. At the end of the story, as their train is about to enter the Saint Gotthard Tunnel, Philip takes his last look at the campanile of Airolo, which in the first chapter he had told Lilia to watch for (it was the beginning of beauty, the promise of the future). But as Philip tries to catch a glimpse of the campanile just before the train plunges into the darkness of the tunnel, he sees "instead the fair myth of Endymion." Caroline Abbott remained a goddess to the last, for to her no love was degrading, since she stood beyond degradation. She lifted him to so great a height that he could tell her that he was her worshiper, like Gino, who also thought her a goddess. "But what was the use of telling her? For all the wonderful things had happened."

Almost all of Forster's values are brought to play in this novel, which foreshadows the rest of his work. Instead of the fantasy of the short stories, however, *Where Angels Fear to Tread* features accident and coincidence. Now and then the careful progress of the plot suffers from an abrupt theatrical interruption. This is sometimes disturbing in a basically realistic story, where the great points should be made through the psychological without too much assistance from the accidental. In "The Story of a Panic," the reader's imagination readily accepts Pan's possession of the soul of the boy Eustace, and the boy's subsequent ecstatic rush to the woodland. In Forster's first novel, Gino's violence is plausible, and it gives him a certain fierce reality, but the arrival of Caroline Abbott just in time to rescue Philip seems a little pat, coming as it does so soon after the accident in which Gino's baby has been killed. These are minor objections, however, in the face of the story's achievements, its remarkable maturity as a first novel. Philip's sudden realization of his love for Caroline, and her spasmodic admission of her feelings toward Gino, may seem to match the abruptness of some of the outer effects, but actually these onsets of love are substantially motivated, proceeding out of events. The characters are all well drawn, and Gino is Forster's most successful attempt at portraying the child of nature. Forster gives the travelogue element just the right amount of color, and he devises certain episodes with notable skill. One of these is the performance of the provincial Italian opera company, at which Harriet behaves with prissiness and Gino with uproarious geniality. This is an important moment in the expansion of Philip's character: he is on Gino's side here rather than Harriet's.

As usual in Forster, the story contains a conflict between two worlds, as represented by the English town of Sawston (which Philip finally comes around to calling "that hole") and the Italian town of Monteriano (which in Forster's parody of Baedeker is described as "now of small importance, and seat of the district prison. The inhabitants are still noted for their agreeable manners"). But Forster, even as a young novelist of only twenty-six, shrewdly avoided oversimplification in his opposition of these two places, these two ways of life: he turned the full dry light of social comedy on Monteriano as well as on Sawston. Granted, Monteriano comes off better; but Forster never suggests that it is perfect or utopian.

Philip Herriton and Caroline Abbott are characters of the kind that Forster, years later (not speaking of his own work), would designate as round: they change, they are capable of surprising the reader. Caroline is young, in her early twenties, and it is doubtful that she will remain forever on the shelf because of Gino. For one thing, the episode in which she bathes his brown baby indicates her talent for motherhood. As for Philip, the experiences he has gone through with Caroline have restored his sense of beauty and presumably will restore his sense of humor. At the end of the book he has decided to leave Sawston, for London. He would probably choose Monteriano if he could, but he has to make his living in London. At least he is abandoning Sawston and the values represented by his mother and sister. He tells Caroline Abbott that he is nothing more than a spectator of life, but surely he will from now on be a better and wiser spectator and possibly, at necessary times, a participant.

In *The Longest Journey* (1907), the detestable Sawston appears again. It gives its name to the middle section of the novel, whose first part takes its title from enlightened Cambridge and its third from pagan Wiltshire. Rickie Elliot, the sensitive, clubfooted young man, has in childhood lost his unlikable father and his lovable mother in a few terse sentences (Rickie's own death will be described later with almost equal abruptness). Living in Sawston after the university, Rickie speaks to his wife Agnes of his time at Cambridge: "those are the magic years, and—with luck—you see up there what you couldn't see before and mayn't ever see again." Rickie's philosophical friend, Stewart Ansell, had not "seen" Agnes when she had visited Cambridge long before there was a possibility of marriage with Rickie. When she appeared at Cambridge, Ansell ignored her outstretched hand, and when Rickie later scolded him privately for his rudeness, Ansell said no one had been there. When Rickie reminded Ansell that he had "seen" a philosophic cow during a dialectical dispute, Ansell retorted that there are two kinds of phenomena: "*one*, those which have a real existence, such as the cow; *two*, those which are the subjective product of a diseased imagination, and which, to our destruction, we invest with the semblance of reality." But Rickie ignored this warning, and after Agnes's athletic hero,

Gerald, an officer and a bully, was killed (in two sentences) at a Rugby match, Rickie struck precisely the right sympathetic note, and before long he and Agnes were married.

At Sawston, where Agnes's brother, Herbert Pembroke, finds him a teaching position, Rickie deteriorates. The school is a reflection of the Tonbridge where Forster was so unhappy as a boy. (Forster in 1920, in his *Abinger Harvest* essay "Notes on the English Character" wrote that the institution of public schools produced men with "undeveloped hearts.") At Sawston, Agnes gives birth to a little girl, who has Rickie's physical defect; but the child is exterminated in another of those one-sentence deaths ("After a short, painless illness, his daughter died"). Rickie, whose disillusionment with Agnes has grown, comes to see her as Ansell had: "Like the world she had created for him, she was unreal." Rickie has meanwhile acquired another relative. His aunt has told him that the hearty, crude young man she has brought up—Stephen Wonham—is Rickie's half brother.

Agnes persuades Rickie not to tell Stephen this. Rickie dislikes him because he thinks his own father was also Stephen's, but eventually he feels Stephen must be told: "The lie we acted has ruined our lives," he says to Agnes. But he still makes no move toward Stephen. Then Ansell, who has for the second and implacably final time failed to get his Cambridge fellowship—it is one of Forster's little jokes to have the tutors say that Ansell had read too much Hegel—bursts into Sawston School. Rickie, Agnes, Herbert, the masters, and the boys are all in the dining hall when Ansell makes a great trumpeting revelation, not only that Rickie has a bastard brother whom he will not acknowledge, but also that this half brother is the son of Rickie's mother. It is an effectively dramatic scene, the voice of Cambridge, with all the righteousness of the twisted Gregors Werle in Ibsen's *The Wild Duck,* shouting out the

[23]

uncomfortable truth to hypocritical Sawston. Amid the tumult, Rickie faints, as he had when he first heard about Stephen's relationship to him—presumably on the hated paternal side.

Now Rickie feels differently about his mother's other son; he leaves Agnes and goes to live in Wiltshire with Stephen, who greets him sullenly. He and Rickie are not attuned—Rickie is particularly repelled by Stephen's heavy drinking—but they remain together. One night, however, when he learns that Stephen is drunk after promising "to behave decently," Rickie feels that for the second time in his life he has gone bankrupt: "Pretended again that people were real. May God have mercy on me!" Finding Stephen lying in a stupor across a railway track, he just has time to push him out of the way before a train comes. But he cannot save himself. And in a final chapter set several years in the future, Stephen is married and a father, living on the soil as a farmer. In a scene of ironic comedy, he haggles with Herbert Pembroke, now a clergyman, over Rickie's literary remains. For Rickie had written some stories, which he could not sell during his lifetime but which have become popular after his death. They are little fantasies, one of them about a girl changing into a tree.

In *The Longest Journey*, the portraits of Rickie, Ansell, Agnes, and others are expertly achieved: they come up from the page as believable. Stephen Wonham alone seems difficult to accept as actual. Rather extravagantly called Siegfried in the first draft of the story, Stephen is a far less successful attempt at a child of nature than Gino Carella in the previous novel. Forster was able to catch all the exotic phases of Gino and make them credible, while Gino's quick outburst of cruelty added to his vitality. With Stephen, Forster—who did so well with a variety of people—is not quite able to convey the quality of the English boor: he seems to fall between idealizing him and portraying him realistically, and never quite brings these two phases together into a living characterization. Otherwise the book is finely wrought, with people once again representing places and ideas and yet for the most part behaving as individual human beings rather than as types. Cambridge will not mix with Sawston, nor Cambridge and Sawston with Wiltshire; and Rickie, torn by the three of them, pays a heavy price. His life is so miserable that his death comes almost as a relief to the reader.

Although the book presents a number of its important events as headlines rather than as developed dramatic episodes, it contains some excitingly good scenes, such as Ansell's giving out the truth in the school dining hall. There are bits of social comedy and shrewd observation learned from Jane Austen and Samuel Butler, who with Proust, Forster says, "have helped me most over my writing." Because the first part of Proust's novel was not published until 1913, he cannot be counted as an influence before *A Passage to India;* Forster has said that Butler "did more than the other two to help me look at life the way I do. What is that way? It is the undogmatic way." Forster has further said that from Jane Austen he "learned the possibilities of domestic humour." It should perhaps be pointed out that these writers are only partial influences on Forster, and not obstacles to his originality. One of the phases of technique, for example, which he shares with Proust (and mentions in *Aspects of the Novel*) is the leitmotiv, which Forster in speaking of Proust's handling of the "Venteuil" sonata designates as a component of rhythm. In his early period, Forster was already making use of such devices. Consider the Hermes statue in *The Longest Journey*, a figure associated with both Gerald and Stephen. And the one picture in Stephen's room is, perhaps a bit too poetically, of Demeter, goddess of grain.

But there is a more complicated example of rhythm in this sense: the pictures in Rickie's Cambridge room in the first chapter. These are more than static symbols; they keep turning up as themselves or in variations, and have therefore a

[25]

kinetic function. One of them is George Frederick Watts's "Sir Percival," another is "a cheap brown madonna," still another is what some visitors assume is Venice but the informed know to be Stockholm; and there is a picture of Rickie's mother, "looking rather sweet." What the "Sir Percival" stands for we learn at the end of the sixteenth chapter, when Rickie, hurt by a magazine editor's rejection of his stories, is planning to marry Agnes and teach at Sawston: "Rickie trusted that to him also benefits might accrue; that his wound might heal as he laboured, and his eyes recapture the Holy Grail." As for his "cheap" religious painting, Rickie discovers that the superior Pembrokes have "madonnas of acknowledged merit"; this is not emphasized, only mentioned, but it points up some differences. Rickie does not know of his mother's escapade in Stockholm with the man who became Stephen's father, but this is undoubtedly the source of the picture of that city, near which Mrs. Elliot's Wiltshire-farmer lover drowned. In the last scene the picture is in Stephen's possession, and Herbert Pembroke accuses him of causing it "to be filched from the walls of my house." The photograph of the mother had turned up somewhat earlier, when Rickie held it out to Stephen as a bond between them, and Stephen, who wanted to be loved for himself, not out of relationship, tore the picture to pieces. The use to which these objects are put indicates Forster's method of expanding a story, deepening it, getting beyond the usual effects of plot and character by means of what he was later to define as rhythm.

His third novel to be published, *A Room with a View* (1908), was begun before the other two: "The Italian half of the novel was almost the first piece of fiction I attempted. I laid it aside to write and publish two other novels, and then returned to it and added the English half." It is lighter than the other two books, and Forster has called it his "nicest" novel.

It begins in a Florentine pensione he calls the Bertolini,

which was actually the Simi, on the Lungarno alle Grazie (as E. M. Forster has said in a letter, "It no longer exists, though the building itself has not been destroyed. It faces San Miniato. A pensione on the other [San Miniato] side of the river is sometimes—and wrongly—pointed out as its origin"). The story begins with confusion at the Bertolini: a young English girl, Lucy Honeychurch, and her elderly cousin-companion, Charlotte Bartlett, are unhappy when they arrive and find that they will not have the rooms which had been promised them overlooking the Arno. "I have a view, I have a view," a heavily built old man in the dining room cries out, insisting that they change rooms with him and his son George. Miss Bartlett tries to freeze out old Mr. Emerson, but without success, so the two sets of people make the transfer. The Emersons will from now on play an important part in Lucy's life: when she sees a murder committed in the Piazza della Signoria, the arms she falls back into are those of George Emerson; and on an excursion to Fiesole, when she stumbles down a little hillside onto a terrace full of violets, George is standing there and promptly embraces and kisses her. Before Lucy has a chance to react, a voice calls her name three times: "The silence of life had been broken by Miss Bartlett, who stood brown against the view."

Back in England at her home, Windy Corner, Lucy becomes engaged to Cecil Vyse. He is medieval and "like a Gothic statue" (Forster dislikes the Middle Ages). But George Emerson and his father appear as householders in the Honeychurches' town in Surrey, and George takes another occasion to kiss Lucy, this time in the garden of her home. She rebuffs him, but that evening she breaks her engagement with Cecil, who could conceive only a feudal relationship, "that of protector and protected. He had no glimpse of the comradeship after which the girl's soul yearned." Later, old Mr. Emerson, who is childishly outspoken, pleads with Lucy on behalf of his son—and successfully. The story ends at the Bertolini, where

George and Lucy have a room with a view. Happiness spreads before them, and even Miss Bartlett, whom Lucy speaks of as "dreadful frozen Charlotte," turns out not to be so bad after all, for George tells his bride that it was Charlotte who made possible the important interview between Lucy and the elder Emerson which resulted in the marriage: "from the very first moment we met, she hoped, far down in her mind, that we should be like this . . ."

It is a crowded little comedy, but less complex and involved than the other two books. Some of the names of the people virtually suggest Restoration plays: not only Lucy Honeychurch, but the Reverend Mr. Eager and the lady novelist, Eleanor Lavish. Mr. Emerson, the loud humanist, may be mischievously named in parody of the ideals of self-reliance, friendship, compensation, and English traits. Yet, for all its sharpness as a comedy, *A Room with a View* has a thin quality. As social comedy, it lacks a rape-of-the-lock satiric sting, nor is it a vital picture of pride and prejudice melting before love. There is one unlikable clergyman, Mr. Eager, and a halfway unlikable one, Mr. Beebe, and in Victorian fashion there are little interpolated sermons and editorials by the author, as in his two earlier novels. Here, no atmospheres clash, as in the other books, though the influence of Tuscany seems more beneficent than that of Surrey.

A number of characters in the book fail to establish concord, especially Lucy and Cecil. The latter is somewhat on the order of Philip Herriton in *Where Angels Fear to Tread*. In the important moments, however, people do manage to communicate: George with his impulsive kisses, and his somewhat grotesque father with the ability to find just the right words to say to Lucy as she is about to leave for Greece. But none of these characters have the energetic attractiveness of several in the earlier novels (Caroline Abbott, Gino Carella, even the weak but sympathetic Rickie Elliot), or of so many of them in the later books. George Emerson, for all his ardor and energy, is moody and rather commonplace, though he shows promise at the end with his discerning remarks about Charlotte Bartlett. Lucy is a likable, ordinary, attractive girl, but not one with the luminous quality of the sharp-witted Elizabeth Bennett of *Pride and Prejudice*.

Perhaps the strongest social-comedy element in *A Room with a View* is the opposition of the lower-middle-class Emersons with the upper-middle-class Cecil Vyse and his public-school background; but if Cecil is, in Lucy's eyes, limited to the medieval and the feudal, George Emerson has some of the eager vitality of the Renaissance, though without its classical learning or abundant creativity—yet he is right for Lucy, that admirer of Italy and the Renaissance, so the story as it works out is Forster's happiest, most optimistic novel.

Forster had a bit of fun imagining the future of these characters when, in 1958, to celebrate the fiftieth birthday of *A Room with a View*, he wrote an "Anniversary Postscript," for *The Observer*. George and Lucy, Forster imagines, would have settled in Highgate. ("Lucy . . . must now be in her late sixties, George in his early seventies—a ripe age though not as ripe as my own. They are still a personable couple, and fond of each other and of their children and grandchildren.") George, who had worked his way into a well-paid government clerkship, would have become a conscientious objector in World War I. Lucy, who insisted on playing Beethoven ("Hun music!"), received a call from the police, apparently at the instigation of neighbors. (When old Mr. Emerson, who lived with his son and daughter-in-law, lectured the policeman, they warned him. He died soon afterward, "still looking out and confident that Love and Truth would see humanity through in the end.") At the outbreak of World War II, George at the age of fifty enlisted at once because, "being intelligent and passionate, he could distinguish between a Germany that was not much worse than England and a Germany that was devilish." After being taken prisoner in Africa, George was removed to southern Italy, and when the Italian government collapsed he visited Florence on his way north. Although the city had been somewhat damaged, the Bertolini area was untouched, but the Bertolini itself was gone, changed, some of the façades shrunken or extended, so that George had

to report to Lucy that the View was still there and that the Room must be there too but could not be found. She was glad of the news, although at that moment she was homeless and possessionless. It was something to have retained a View, and secure in it and in their love as long as they have one another to love, George and Lucy await the Third World War—the one that would end war and everything else too.

Forster ends his amusing little epilogue with a note on Cecil Vyse, who in 1914 "was seconded to Information or whatever the withholding of information was then entitled." At a party Forster attended in the outskirts of Alexandria during the war, the hostess was reluctant to have Beethoven played, but a young officer spoke up and said that someone who knew about such things had assured him that Beethoven was really a Belgian. The young officer was almost certainly Cecil, for "that mixture of mischief and culture is unmistakable. Our hostess was reassured, the ban was lifted, and the Moonlight Sonata shimmered into the desert."

In 1910, two years after publication of *A Room with a View*, *Howards End* appeared. It was a new Forster; he had arrived at his major phase as a novelist.

Howards End, one of the most famous of symbolic houses in English literature, was an actual place that a family of Howards once owned. Forster lived in this Hertfordshire house from the time he was four until he was fourteen. He says in

[30]

Marianne Thornton that "the garden, the overhanging wych-elm, the sloping meadow, the great view to the west, the adjacent farm through the high tangled hedge of wild roses were all utilized by me in *Howards End,* and the interior is in the novel too." Forster had hoped to live and die there: "It certainly was a lovable little house, and still is, though it now stands just outside a twentieth-century hub and almost within sound of a twentieth-century hum."

In the novel, the first Mrs. Wilcox grew up there; she is of the yeoman stock Forster so much admires, and like Mrs. Moore in *A Passage to India,* she is a grand elderly woman whose influence lingers after her death. Before dying, she writes a note saying that she wants Howards End left to her younger friend Margaret Schlegel, but her family regards this bequest as an aberration and finds excuses to ignore it ("not legally binding"). The husband, Henry Wilcox, and his brutal and violent elder son Charles, are of the world of business and practicality, and although they have no proper feeling for Howards End, they cling to it.

Margaret Schlegel and her sister Helen represent a way of life opposite to that of the male Wilcoxes, with one of whom, Paul, Helen is briefly and embarrassingly involved at the beginning of the story. The late father of the Schlegel girls had left Germany because of his disgust with the materialist outlook, the militarist character, and the imperialist ambitions of the newly federated nation. The girls represent what was later to be called "the other Germany": the cultural side, particularly the musical. It is at a performance of Beethoven's Fifth Symphony that they meet Leonard Bast, a physically and spiritually undernourished young London clerk who is a walking testimonial to the fact that even the famous liberal reform movements of the nineteenth century had not, by the twentieth, done much toward alleviating the conditions one of Benjamin Disraeli's characters spoke of in 1845 in the novel *Sybil, or the Two Nations.* The "two nations" were the rich and the poor,

between whom there is no intercourse and no sympathy; who are as ignorant of each other's habits, thoughts and feelings, as if they were dwellers in different zones, or inhabitants of different planets; who are formed by a different breeding, are fed by a different food, are ordered by different manners and are not governed by the same laws.

Forster, in describing Leonard Bast, says he did not belong to "the very poor," but "he knew that he was poor, and would admit it: he would have died sooner than admit any inferiority to the rich." So he reads Ruskin and attends concerts at Queen's Hall.

The Schlegel girls take him up seriously, and upon learning from Henry Wilcox that the insurance company which employs Leonard Bast might fail, they persuade him to leave it. At a lower salary, he goes to work in a bank, which soon lets him go in an employment reduction. Meanwhile, Henry Wilcox has proposed to Margaret and been accepted. At the wedding of Wilcox's daughter Evie, at his country house in Shropshire, Helen Schlegel suddenly appears with Leonard Bast and his wife Jacky, a blowsy slattern a dozen years older than he is. The Basts have been reduced to desperation because of the business advice, channeled through the Schlegels, that Henry Wilcox does not even remember giving. Helen has come down like an avenging angel to put matters right. Margaret shunts them all off to the village inn, but Jacky stays behind and gets drunk on the wedding wine. She encounters Henry, whom she addresses as Hen, and Margaret discovers that, years before, Jacky had been his mistress. Margaret decides not to let this stand between herself and Henry, and subsequently marries him.

Later, when Helen, back from a trip to the Continent, will communicate with Margaret only through letters, Henry and

Margaret lure her to Howards End by telling her that the Schlegels' possessions are there and that she must unpack her books. Surprising Helen at the house, Margaret sees that she is pregnant. Helen wants to stay with the familiar furniture that night at Howards End—Margaret and Henry are located nearby at Charles's, but she wants Margaret to join her for that night, after which Helen will go to Munich for the birth of her child. Henry refuses: "Helen commands my sympathy . . . But I cannot treat her as if nothing had happened." Margaret goes to stay with her anyhow, and plans to leave her husband forever. That night she hears from Helen of her one joyless night with Leonard Bast, in Shropshire, at the time of Evie's wedding. Leonard, who does not know of the impending child, feels guilty because he has been Helen's lover and goes to Howards End to look for Margaret and confess that he is sorry. Leonard, like Stephen Wonham, becomes increasingly unreal: perhaps because of class differences in Victorian and Edwardian England, Forster could not have known such men well, as he apparently knew Italians and Indians in their own countries. Leonard in any event has been more than anything else an emblematic figure: when first introduced, he has an umbrella that is "all gone along the seams." But on his fatal visit to Howards End the symbols multiply. As he enters the house in the early morning he meets Charles, who has learned of what has happened: Charles seizes from its hanging place on the wall an old sword that had belonged to the Schlegel girls' father, and beats Leonard with it. Leonard falls, killed not by the sword but by a weak heart. As he crumples to the floor he catches hold of a bookcase, which is upset, showering books over him. It is a sword wielded by one of the Wilcoxes, the new conquerors of England, which has in effect killed Leonard, and it is the books of the Schlegels, representative of the culture he has aspired to, which symbolically bury him.

Although the autopsy shows that Leonard Bast was in the

last stages of heart disease, Charles is tried and sentenced to three years' imprisonment for manslaughter. Margaret had told her husband that she planned to take Helen to Germany and stay there with her after the birth of the child, but when Henry turns to her pathetically after Charles is sentenced, Margaret goes with Henry to Howards End, to help him recover. At the end of the book he has called a family council there and told his children that he will leave them all his money, but that Howards End will go to Margaret, who learns for the first time, from something she overhears, that Mrs. Wilcox had wanted her to have the place. After her own death, it will become the property of her nephew—Leonard Bast's son—now a tiny child out in the adjoining fields with Helen, who on the last page of the novel bursts into the house rejoicing because there will be a great crop of hay.

Hay is one of the important symbols of *Howards End:* both the earlier Mrs. Wilcox and Margaret are associated with it. The former is introduced into the story with her hands full of hay, and Margaret several times twines grass in her own hands. In contrast to this, the male Wilcoxes are victims of hay fever. There are other suggestive images, such as the wych-elm mentioned in the earlier quotation by Forster describing the house that served as the original for Howards End: in an interview he said that this tree is symbolic, "the genius of the house," which itself stands for the enduring England (as Lionel Trilling was the first to point out). Today, this England is being cut down and cut up; Forster has been quoted earlier in a 1956 reference to "the twentieth-century hum" near the original Howards End, a reference he expanded three years later in a BBC broadcast ("Recollections of Nassenheide"), in which he said, "The tragedy of England is that she is too small to become a modern state and yet to retain her freshness. The freshness has to go." The loss of the freshness is accompanied by the loss of "the heritage which I used to see from my own doorstep in Hertfordshire when I was a child, and which has failed to outlast me." But even as early as 1910, the year of the novel, outspreading London threatened the peace of the countryside around Howards End: "Henry's kind had filched most of [the glebe]" that should have bordered the length of the Great North Road, on which the new monsters, the automobiles (Henry Wilcox's car is suggested as evil) are bringing to the fresh countryside the mechanization of the city. It is as if the recurrent goblins of Helen Schlegel's vision are taking over, the goblins she finds in the third movement of Beethoven's Fifth Symphony: "The music started with a goblin walking quietly over the universe, from end to end."

The "only connect" idea occurs when Margaret is pondering how she can point out to Henry Wilcox the salvation that is possible from within him and every man: "Only connect the prose and the passion, and both will be exalted, and human love will be seen at its height. Live in fragments no longer. Only connect, and the beast and the monk, robbed of the isolation that is life to either, will die." But she has not counted on Henry's obtuseness; she cannot get her ideas across to him. Throughout, the Schlegels and the Wilcoxes never really connect, though Margaret tries. Helen, early in the story, says that the Wilcoxes are "just a wall of newspapers and motor-cars and golf-clubs," and she is sure that behind that wall only emptiness and panic exist. Margaret tells her that "there is a great outer life" which she and Helen do not know, "in which telegrams and anger count." In it, personal relations do not govern, and love there "means marriage settlements, death, death duties." But "though obviously horrid," this outer life "often seems the real one—there's grit in it. It does breed character." Margaret tends throughout to defend the male Wilcoxes, and at one point she tells Helen that, without such men, "there would be no trains, no ships to carry us literary people about in, no fields even. Just savagery." The opposition between the Schlegel and Wilcox ways of life is somewhat thrown out of balance by Margaret's eagerness to connect. Forster skillfully has avoided an exactly balanced antithesis: rather he has presented a series of uncoordinated opposites.

As noted earlier, Henry's rigidity breaks whatever connection has been in the process of becoming established, and Margaret prepares to leave him. But she stays with him when she sees that he is shattered by the disgrace over Charles, and it is as a sick man that Henry lives at Howards End with her and Helen and the Bast child—a sick man, though not altogether a discontented one. Nevertheless, the true connection that Margaret had hoped for is not made. She has merely triumphed because of circumstances. She indulges in a rare moment of private gloating after Henry has announced that Howards End will be hers: "She, who had never expected to conquer anyone, had charged straight through these Wilcoxes and broken up their lives." This stresses breaking, not connecting—breaking followed by submission. But ultimately all will be well at Howards End, except for the encroachment of the symbolically evil city, and the child of Leonard Bast will inherit this earth. Leonard, ruined by the city, was two generations removed from the soil; his son, also the son of the cultivated Helen Schlegel, will settle into the life known by the family of the first Mrs. Wilcox, whose magic touch has made possible a hopeful future.

Forster's gifts of comedy and irony are again manifest, as well as the simple strength of his style, which in the present book ranges on the edge of the poetic, sometimes dangerously so. Some of the symbols of this novel have been referred to. Most of them are easily discernible, and yet they embody that intuitive quality of the symbolism of the modern school (which, after Baudelaire's pioneering sonnet "Correspondances," might be called correspondential symbolism). The element of the romantic in Forster's fiction, so often neglected in discussion of his work, appears forcibly in *Howards End*, not so much in relation to love as in relation to a romantic feeling for the earth, the places on it, and their influence. There is, above all, Howards End itself, the center of sanctification for both Mrs. Wilcoxes. It is a way of life upon the earth.

The usual critical dispute about Forster's last two novels is whether *Howards End* or *A Passage to India* is the best of all his books. His own preference is for *The Longest Journey*, perhaps because of his affinity with Rickie Elliot, who of all Forster characters is the one temperamentally closest to his author. In any dispute over the relative merits of *Howards End* and *A Passage to India*, it might be noted that each book is extremely excellent in its own way. *Howards End*, which is the only Forster novel apart from *The Longest Journey* whose action takes place entirely inside England, has an enriching complexity, but its theme can be understood without too much difficulty. *A Passage to India*, the only one of the novels set entirely outside England, has its own complexities and contains a mystery not too easy to resolve. As a novel, however, it is more satisfactory than any of the others, for a number of reasons. For one thing, it has more dramatization (and significant description that bears on the action) and fewer editorial comments than all the rest. More important, all its characters, English and Indian, are convincing: there are no imperfections in the portraiture such as there were in the instances of Stephen Wonham and Leonard Bast. And because the people of *A Passage to India* fuse so readily with theme and plot, the book is satisfactory in a way that no other Forster novel is: he had achieved a mastery of the medium. And yet, published more

[37]

than forty years ago, it is still his latest novel to appear in print. Why he stopped writing fiction in mid-career, at the height of his powers, has been one of the great literary puzzles of the age. As to why he ceased producing novels, Forster told Angus Wilson in a 1957 interview, "I just drifted out of it."

Before *Howards End*, Forster had begun a novel he never completed, *Arctic Summer*:

I had got my antithesis all right, the antithesis between the civilized man, who hopes for an Arctic summer in which there is time to get things done, and the heroic man. But I had not settled what is going to happen, and that is why the novel remains a fragment.

Late in 1910, after *Howards End* had come out, Forster made notes for a novel about a large and varied family; the setting was to be the English countryside and perhaps Paris. But he soon noted that he was too "tired" to write this. In 1911, the year he brought out *The Celestial Omnibus*, he tried his hand at what he has called "a bad unpublished play," *The Heart of Bosnia*. At another time, influenced by reading Anatole France, Forster attempted a novel about the Renaissance, but it remained unfinished. There are rumors, however, of a completed novel to be published sometime in the future.

As for *A Passage to India*, Forster had difficulties with it over a number of years. He began it in England after the 1912–13 visit to India, and then the war intervened. When he returned to that country in 1922, he took with him the chapters he had written, but discovered that he could not work on the book there: "What I had written wasn't India at all. It was sticking a photograph on a picture. However, I couldn't *write* it when I was in India. When I got away, I could get on with it." But he "still thought the book bad, and probably should not have completed it without the encouragement of Leonard Woolf."

A piquant introduction to the problems, as well as to the

setting, of *A Passage to India* occurs in a book Forster brought out just twenty-nine years after the novel. *The Hill of Devi* (1953) is an account of his first two trips to India, in 1912–13 and 1922. It is made up largely of letters written to his mother and friends in England, chiefly concerning the Maharajah of Dewas Senior. He is "a bright and tiny young Indian" in the 1912–13 letters, and in those of 1922 a mature ruler with a sense of humor and a longing for affection. He could never be disturbed during his two-hour period of prayer: "I am so very sorry I am holy just now." Forster found on his first visit that "this amazing little state" could "have no parallel, except in a Gilbert and Sullivan opera." But during the six months of his second stay, which he could have made permanent but chose not to, Forster sank sympathetically into the place and its affairs.

The longest section of the book, "Gokul Ashtami," describes the festival of that name which Forster attended for nine days; it gave him the scenery of the Shri Krishna ceremonies in the last part of *A Passage to India*. He closes *The Hill of Devi* with an account of the last unhappy years of the Maharajah, whose son and heir fled from Dewas in 1927 because he thought his father was trying to poison him. This scandal intensified various political troubles the Maharajah was undergoing; in 1933 he left Dewas to live in Pondicherry, capital of French India, where he was a stranger. He prayed and fasted until his death in 1937.

Forster rounds off his notable portrait of this man by saying that it is impossible to think evenly of the dead, who slip out of sight and "go into silence. Yet we cannot help assigning some of them a tune." Usually, people do not leave a sound behind them, and cannot be evoked. But the Maharajah "has the rare quality of evoking himself, and I do not believe that he is here doing it for the last time."

Many interpretations of *A Passage to India* exist, but as in all

Forster's novels the central theme is the inability of human beings to "connect." Here the two conflicting worlds are those of the colonial English and of the native Indian, both Mohammedan and Hindu. Forster in 1957 said that the India he had written of "no longer exists, either politically or socially . . . Assuredly the novel dates." But it distinctly does not, and one of the principal reasons for its continued existence is that in writing it Forster's "main purpose was not political, was not even sociological." He told a miraculously good story of a place and a time, and this should be enough. Criticisms of Forster's historical accuracy such as those made by Nirad C. Chaudhuri in "Passage to and from India" (*Encounter*, June, 1954) are merely literal and specious. For later events have demonstrated that the book is also timely not only for this moment of colonial troubles in different parts of the world and civil-rights uprisings in the United States, but emphatically appropriate on a larger scale because it is a picture of the human condition in our age. *A Passage to India* intensifies the message of *Howards End:* "Only connect."

This might well be the motto of Mrs. Moore, whose influence dominates the book somewhat in the manner of the first Mrs. Wilcox of *Howards End*. Both these elderly women—Mrs. Wilcox dies early in the story she appears in, Mrs. Moore at about the middle of the other novel—have a message that is stated only in action (Mrs. Wilcox's wish to give the house to Margaret Schlegel) or in a few cryptic but significant statements (Mrs. Moore's brief remarks about the innocence of an accused man, made "indifferently" to his accuser and later possibly repeated in her sleep and overheard). Both Mrs. Wilcox and Mrs. Moore are symbolic figures, among other things emblemizing the continuity of underlying truths: continuity, a sustained connection. Their intuitions as human beings are carried over into what they represent, for symbols at their most forceful are connotative rather than denotative and can best be apprehended through intuition. Each of these women is a form of the *magna dea* or *magna mater*, sharing this identity with such quite different women in modern literature as Mrs. Ramsay in Virginia Woolf's *To the Lighthouse* and Molly Bloom in James Joyce's *Ulysses*. Forster in his earlier books had tried with less success to project the intuitive, half-articulate, essentially nonintellectual character (and symbol) in males such as Gino Carella and Stephen Wonham. In his last two novels he succeeds marvelously with Mrs. Wilcox and Mrs. Moore, who even in death pervade the story: Margaret finally acquires Howards End in a way that promises a continuity Mrs. Wilcox could hardly have known, and Mrs. Moore has given Adela Quested the clarity of vision that helps her see truth. There is no easy solution in either case, certainly not in *A Passage to India*, in which the accused man who has been freed remains surly, but in each instance Forster has by indirection, by means of these grand elderly women, pointed a way toward some of the secrets of life, and toward true possibilities of connection.

A Passage to India is divided into three parts ("Mosque," "Caves," "Temple") which Forster says "represent the three seasons of the Cold Weather, the Hot Weather, and the Rains, which divide the Indian year." The central theme of the book concerns the attempts at friendship between the Englishman Cyril Fielding and the Mohammedan Indian Dr. Aziz. The central incidents, which have a drastic effect upon this friendship, are the occurrence at the Marabar caves and the subsequent trial of Dr. Aziz. Delighted to find some English people who are not snobbish, the eager Aziz has invited Fielding to visit the Marabar caves along with two newly arrived Englishwomen: Mrs. Moore, mother of the City Magistrate of Chandrapore, and the plain-looking Adela Quested, who considers marrying Mrs. Moore's son, Ronny Heaslop. Before consenting to a formal engagement, Adela has come out to see him in his new environment. Ronny only expresses the general attitude of the English colony when he disapproves of his mother's and Adela's association with Indians. And certainly the association does lead to catastrophe.

Adela staggers out of one of the caves, and after plunging downhill through cactus, is taken back to Chandrapore in a friend's car. In high hysteria, she says that Dr. Aziz had tried to assault her in the cave. He is arrested, and the antagonism between the English and the Indian sections of the community reaches a boiling point. Fielding, who was not a witness though he was nearby, is ostracized by the English for insisting that Aziz could not have been guilty of the attempted assault. The sibylline Mrs. Moore, also not a witness, likewise believes in the innocence of Aziz, but leaves India before the trial. In dealing with these events, Forster shows the highest skill, brilliantly weaving the narrative through all the complications of the plot. To the admitted earlier influences of Samuel Butler and Jane Austen, Forster had added Proust: "I learned ways of looking at character from him. The modern subconscious way." Proust's writing also confirmed Forster in his use of the leitmotiv, taken from music. Here, such manifestations as the recurring wasp illustrate the technique: Mrs. Moore, seeing it as a creature of essential beauty, at least of prettiness, is close to Dr. Godbole, the Brahman mystic in the story who at the Shri Krishna festival in the last part of the book remembers a wasp he has seen and thinks of it in terms of union with God.

The trial itself is thematically and dramatically powerful, and pungent with humor. When Superintendent of Police McBryde opens the case for the prosecution, he cannot resist the temptation to harp on his favorite belief, "that the darker races are physically attracted by the fairer, but not vice versa," at which a disembodied voice asks, "Even when the lady is so uglier than the gentleman?" At once a native policeman seizes an Indian who had said nothing, and hustles him out of the courtroom. Later the name of Mrs. Moore is invoked: why had the prosecution got her out of the way so that she could not testify on behalf of Aziz? The native crowd begins to chant, "Esmiss Esmoor," horrifying Ronny, who does not want his mother transformed by parody into a Hindu goddess. No one there knows that Mrs. Moore has died on the ship taking her toward England. Some of her spirit may have infused itself into Miss Quested, who when called upon to testify, drily says that it was all a mistake, that Aziz did not follow her into the cave. Aziz is freed amid uproar. Adela Quested, cut off from the English colony and in possible danger of violence from the Indians, takes refuge in the school Fielding directs. After she leaves India there is a rumor that she and Fielding have been lovers there. Aziz accepts this preposterous story as fact: an intricately complicated human being, he can be a sweet and gentle friend or a little monster.

When Fielding and Aziz meet again two years later, Aziz commits another mistake by thinking that the wife Fielding has brought with him on an official visit to Mau (in Central India, where Aziz has moved) is the former Adela Quested. But he learns that Fielding's wife is Mrs. Moore's daughter, Stella. Fielding and Aziz go for a last ride together, and Aziz is full of hatred for the English and full of prophecy: when the next European war comes, and England is in trouble, "Aha! aha! Then is our time." India will be free. Fielding, now "acquiring some of [the] limitations" of Anglo-India, mocks him, but Aziz says that every Englishman will be driven into the sea, and after that he and Fielding can be friends. Fielding, leaning out of his saddle to hold him affectionately, asks why they cannot be friends now: they both want it. The closing passage of the book says:

But the horses didn't want it—they swerved apart; the earth didn't want it, sending up rocks through which riders must pass single file; the temples, the tank, the jail, the palace, the birds, the carrion, the Guest House, that came into view as they issued from the gap and saw Mau beneath: they didn't want it, they said in their hundred voices, "No, not yet," and the sky said, "No, not there."

The spirit of Mrs. Moore, that woman who was so beneficent yet so imperfect, has not prevailed here, and the two worlds remain apart. The causes are deeper than the experience at the caves, yet ultimately it is that which has made Aziz what he is. Even after Miss Quested has gamely uttered her public retraction, to Aziz she remains a hag, and he says he would have been spared much grief if he had become anti-English long before.

But what had happened in the Marabar caves? Some commentators have made much of the echo both Mrs. Moore and Miss Quested heard there. The "boum," "bou-oum," or "ouboum" may indeed represent the Brahman word "Aum," on which those seeking a mystic transport must meditate. Although Forster never directly says what happened in the cave, it is safe to assume a religious manifestation. The discussions between Fielding and Adela Quested after she has admitted her mistake have a comic irony about them. Fielding, the acknowledged atheist, can see the incident, if it really was an incident, only as a hallucination. Miss Quested, whose ears have stopped ringing with the cave echoes since her testimony at the trial, tells Fielding she may have been frightened by a native guide. When she tries to say that Mrs. Moore knew by telepathy what had happened, or not happened, Fielding makes her drop that word telepathy, and she is only too glad to join in his rationalism. Aziz assumes a point of view that can be called Freudian: when Fielding tries to persuade him to accept an apology rather than instigate a suit for damages, Aziz sneeringly wonders whether Miss Quested will sign an apology saying, "Dear Dr. Aziz, I wish you had come into the cave; I am an awful old hag, and it is my last chance." But did not Forster, in the cave episode, draw once again upon the supernatural, in a country so full of belief in the supernatural? Was not some native god determined to keep his people and the conquering English apart? The last paragraph of the novel says something like this, with both the Indian land and the Indian sky confirming the split between Fielding and Aziz, which is also the split between their two national groups.

And the world of the twentieth century, with its savage wars, confirms this further, since these conflicts are essentially the magnification of individual differences: for what have the wars been fought, and were the things they were fought for worth fighting for? Democracy, which has been on the defensive, would answer in the affirmative, and Forster's work has again and again celebrated the good points of democracy. Yet within the framework of the system itself, individual human beings are unable to "connect." E. M. Forster's novels have given us an important vision of this failure. They are art, first of all, a recording and a projecting of life, but they have looked deeply enough into life to be also prophetic, and importantly so. They have accomplished this with comedy, pathos, romance, and irony, and with an implicit sense of the tragic, for they have shown what Zeus in the *Iliad* calls blindness of heart when he says that the gods should not be blamed by mortals for the trouble they have brought upon themselves through their own blindness of heart. It is just such human weakness that Forster deals with, always keeping the accent on the human, on the behavior of individual human beings. Of all imaginative works in English in this century, Forster's stand highest among those which may properly be called humanistic.

[45]

SELECTED BIBLIOGRAPHY

NOTE: * *means reprinted in* The Collected Tales; † *means reprinted in* Abinger Harvest; ‡ *means reprinted in* Two Cheers for Democracy; § *means reprinted in* Marianne Thornton.

PRINCIPAL WORKS OF E. M. FORSTER

Where Angels Fear to Tread. Edinburgh and London, William Blackwood and Sons, 1905; New York, Alfred A. Knopf, 1920.

The Longest Journey. Edinburgh and London, William Blackwood and Sons, 1907; New York, Alfred A. Knopf, 1922.

A Room with a View. London, Edward Arnold, 1908; New York, Alfred A. Knopf, 1923.

Howards End. London, Edward Arnold, 1910; New York, Alfred A. Knopf, 1921.

*The Celestial Omnibus and Other Stories. London, Sidgwick and Jackson, 1911; New York, Alfred A. Knopf, 1923.

*The Story of the Siren. Richmond, Hogarth Press, 1920.

Notes on Egypt. London, The Labour Research Department [1921]. ("The Government of Egypt: Recommendations by a Committee of the International Section of the Labour Research Department, with Notes on Egypt, by E. M. Forster.")

Alexandria: A History and a Guide. Alexandria, Whitehead Morris, 1922; New York, Doubleday, 1961.

Pharos and Pharillon. Richmond, and London, Hogarth Press, 1923; New York, Alfred A. Knopf, 1923.

A Passage to India. London, Edward Arnold, 1924; New York, Harcourt, Brace, 1924.

†Anonymity: An Enquiry. London, Hogarth Press, 1925.

Aspects of the Novel. London, Edward Arnold, 1927; New York, Harcourt, Brace, 1927.

†The Eternal Moment and Other Stories. London, Sidgwick and Jackson, 1928; New York, Harcourt, Brace, 1928.

†A Letter to Mandan Blanchard. London, Hogarth Press, 1931.

†The Pageant of Abinger. London, Athenaeum Press, 1934.

Goldsworthy Lowes Dickinson. London, Edward Arnold, 1934.

Abinger Harvest. London, Edward Arnold, 1936; New York, Harcourt, Brace, 1936.

[46]

Reading as Usual. Tottenham, Tottenham Public Library, 1939.
†What I Believe. London, Hogarth Press, 1939.
England's Pleasant Land: A Pageant Play. London, Hogarth Press, 1940.
Nordic Twilight. London, Macmillan, 1940.
‡Virginia Woolf. Cambridge, Cambridge University Press, 1942.
‡The Development of English Prose Between 1918 and 1939. Glasgow, Jackson, Son and Co., 1945.
The Collected Tales of E. M. Forster. New York, Alfred A. Knopf, 1947. (In London, as Collected Short Stories, Sidgwick and Jackson, 1947.)
Two Cheers for Democracy. London, Edward Arnold, 1951; New York, Harcourt, Brace, 1951.
Desmond McCarthy. Stanford Dingley, Mill House Press, 1952.
The Hill of Devi. London, Edward Arnold, 1953; New York, Harcourt, Brace, 1953.
§Battersea Rise. New York, Harcourt, Brace [1955].
Marianne Thornton: A Domestic Biography, 1797–1887. London, Edward Arnold, 1956; New York, Harcourt, Brace, 1956.

CRITICAL WORKS AND COMMENTARY

Beer, J. B. The Achievement of E. M. Forster. London, Chatto and Windus, 1962.
Brown, E. K. Rhythm in the Novel. Toronto, University of Toronto Press, 1950.
Burra, Peter. "Introduction" to A Passage to India. London, J. M. Dent and Sons, 1942.
Crews, Frederick C. E. M. Forster: The Perils of Humanism. Princeton, N. J., Princeton University Press, 1962.
Grandsen, K. W. E. M. Forster. Edinburgh, Oliver and Boyd, 1962; New York, Grove Press, 1962.
Johnstone, J. K. The Bloomsbury Group: A Study of E. M. Forster, Lytton Strachey, Virginia Woolf, and Their Circle. New York, The Noonday Press, 1954; London, Secker and Warburg, 1954.
Joseph, David I. The Art of Rearrangement: E. M. Forster's Abinger Harvest. New Haven, Conn., Yale University Press, 1964.
Kirkpatrick, B. J. A Bibliography of E. M. Forster. London, Rupert Hart-Davis, 1965.
Macaulay, Rose. The Writings of E. M. Forster. London, Hogarth Press, 1938; New York, Harcourt, Brace, 1938.

[47]

McConkey, James. The Novels of E. M. Forster. Ithaca, N.Y., Cornell University Press, 1957.

Natwahr-Singh, K., ed. E. M. Forster: A Tribute, with Selections from his Writings on India. New York, Harcourt, Brace and World, 1964.

Oliver, H. J. The Art of E. M. Forster. Melbourne, Melbourne University Press, 1960; London and New York, Cambridge University Press, 1960.

Tindall, William York. The Literary Symbol. New York, Columbia University Press, 1955.

Trilling, Lionel. E. M. Forster. Norfolk, Conn., New Directions, 1943; London, Hogarth Press, 1944.

Warner, Rex. E. M. Forster. London, Longmans, Green, 1950.

Wilde, Alan. Art and Order: A Study of E. M. Forster. New York, New York University Press, 1964.